LEFT FOR RIGHT

Left *for* Right

GLEN DOWNIE

PEDLAR PRESS | *Toronto*

ACKNOWLEDGEMENTS
The publisher wishes to thank the Canada Council for
the Arts and the Ontario Arts Council for their generous
support of our publishing program.

LIBRARY AND ARCHIVES CANADA
CATALOGUING IN PUBLICATION

Downie, Glen
        Left for right / Glen Downie.

Poems.
ISBN 978-1-897141-48-9

    I. Title.

PS8557.O84L43 2012   C811'.54
C2012-901422-2

COVER ART   Emma Downie

DESIGN   Zab Design & Typography, Toronto

TYPEFACE   Garamond

Printed in Canada

THE CANADA COUNCIL | LE CONSEIL DES ARTS
FOR THE ARTS | DU CANADA
SINCE 1957 | DEPUIS 1957

ONTARIO ARTS COUNCIL
CONSEIL DES ARTS DE L'ONTARIO

This is it I say
This is the human condition
this is what it all boils down to
this is the bread and butter
this is the nuts and bolts
this is the crime and punishment
this is the Tom and Jerry

— STUART ROSS

Contents

Domesticity

Creatures

Fables

Things

Disappearances

Domesticity

The glacier knocks in the cupboard,
The desert sighs in the bed,
And the crack in the tea-cup opens
A lane to the land of the dead.
    — W.H. Auden

Domestic

When they ask *Where's your dishwasher*, I say You're looking at
him. Call it atonement for teenage chores I shirked, stabbing
my selfless mother in the heart. I don't mind. It's my bit
for energy conservation. I also use less soap than I used to,
though not for environmental reasons; below clouds of suds,
the waters of domesticity are more dangerous than generally
thought. Carving knives, broken glass — I swear I had more
fingers than this when I started. My hands were certainly
bigger, stronger, more handsome and could do things. I need
only look at these stubby starfish, with their lesser re-grown
digits, to know what thirty-odd years of dishes has cost me.

The Queen

Among powers and principalities, we are less than Luxembourg or Lichtenstein. Our privy council meets in the privy; our cabinet in a cabinet. And she is the infant monarch of this, the smallest country in the world. She rules with the tiniest iron fist; her every utterance, a royal decree.

It's her father's role to carry her throughout the realm to receive the adoration of her subjects, and indeed, she is revered wherever she goes, especially for her courage during the recent hostilities. Our constitution is still unwritten, and it's not clear what it may mean to the State when her aging porter can no longer carry her. We have never had a queen before, and will never have another — so belovéd is she, we cannot conceive of succession.

Being Siamese

Ah, our two-headed days — how I miss them! Me, the long-
legged one, walking us endlessly everywhere, you growing
steadily at my chest, two heads poking out of one coat. A
traffic-stopping marvel. Women too pretty for one man
were madly interested. Each flower had limitless depth, each
pigeon and squirrel was a flurry; patting a dog would keep us
burbling for days. How sweet the strawberry savoured while
dangling over the tiger's jaws! We were Siamese then, till we
fell, fell into the clutches of those educated butchers who cut
you away, oh my heart.

Third and Long

Between those open legs, I called for you, believing our play foolproof. But you came slippery into my hands; I bobbled you, and dropped back, stumbling. The blitz was on, my protection collapsed around me. Had to tuck you in the crook of my arm and run for my life. The hulks were bearing down; I'd surely be creamed before turning the corner. So I let go a Hail Mary and you sailed through the air. Crushed to the turf, I'd become in that moment the little tailor who outsmarts the giant in a stone-throwing contest, secretly hurling a bird who then flies out of sight.

Barometric Pressure

My sculptor friend declares his pre-Christmas sales *a barometer of the economy*. Walking my girl to school, I consider my own barometers: toe poking from my shoe; my mother-bear snarl at some show-off kick-boxing too close.

Midnight, while the family sleeps, I submerge myself in the war. With an egg, an old hand shows the kids what'll happen if we dive too deep. A primal dread at the heart of all submarine dramas, the common nightmare of those who won't live on the surface. With each reel, we sink ever deeper, narrowly evading depth charges. Our vessel's old, the pressure increases and somebody screams *We can't take it!* Pipes burst, rivets shoot off, glass shatters in the dials and everyone remembers the egg. My taste in late movies just another barometer.

Ugly Voice

A choir practices in the church next door at the same hour every week. Great angel wings of sound swoop toward heaven from its open windows. But one struggling voice, deeply flawed, drags down the kite of the soul. I ask myself time and again why no one insists that he mouth the words, why no one points out the obvious, that he can't carry a tune in a bucket. Even with my tin ear, I know he has ruined the effect, that sitting him next to Mr. Perfect Pitch has taught him nothing. I speculate that perhaps he has other problems. That not only is he tone deaf, but otherwise handicapped, or prone to suicidal thoughts, and singing is the saving grace of his life. Nothing gives him greater joy than belting out his tuneless hallelujahs, his wounded bellows of praise. I conclude this is some Christian lesson about acceptance, about all gifts being precious in God's eyes. But what of God's ears? I turn back to my scribbles, soundlessly moving my lips as I struggle to find, within the choir of writers, my lyric voice.

The Break

Twig snapped and dangling, now cast as lumber. Awkward,
oafish, armoured appendage. Like a Brailling forefinger, it
looms disproportionately large in the brain, occupying
space, demanding attention. It claims the pillows on every
couch and bed: a Siamese-twin limb, unlovely growth, a
neurasthenic white elephant. Like the white cliffs of Dover,
it bears the names of sightseers. Precious cargo, delicate relic,
first fall of snow, foretaste of turning to stone.

Big Hand

Each day breaks each night falls o the fragility of time...

    & an impatient child forced to nap *till the big hand reaches*...snaps the big hand off trying to hasten the hour of waking there's so much to do there is kissing there is telling there is the girl next door there are war games nothing casual about casualties don't come crying to me I'll give you something to cry about do you fear the big hand raised the dark basement the unhealthy old book yellow pages brittle & easily torn like lettuce from the moon of course we cry over spilt milk why any other kind of course we count our chickens before during & after of course we are nickelled & dimed to death it's a nice day for a household accident & when we paint ourselves into our lives do we become vivid & animated filling a colouring book with colour or paint ourselves into a corner from which we never escape

    & as though it was time to wake the quaking aspens stood up as one & gave the child a big hand

The Landslide Effect

How dangerous is this springing forward, falling back! To tinker with time, to say it's two when it's one, to go room-to-room resetting this clock and that, and when every alarm, grandfather and wrist has been set, misguidedly, to that same false hour, to not notice those minutes gone lost and the gears lying through their teeth. Does no one consider the consequence of tampering with even a second, of moving one pebble of time on the slippery slope of eternity? How little it takes to trigger the landslide effect that will rumble us as we sleep, so we wake in the morning buried up to our necks in the Pleistocene!

Man Carrying Flowers

A man not wishing to be taken for Miss Kentucky cannot
carry flowers cradled in one arm like a baby. Having bought
them out of love, he must now out of love accept the
attendant public humiliation as he fidgets the long walk
home, trying to balance care with manly disregard. Were he
wealthy, buying pricier blooms, he might insist on a box, and
carry that down the street imagining himself a hit man with a
shotgun hidden among the roses. Or he could toss calla lilies
heedlessly in the back of his Lexus and zoom away, immune.
But he has no car, barely money enough for daisies, so must
parade his love nakedly down the street. Perhaps, like the
youngest member of a wedding party, he thrusts it fixedly
out in front, far from his body, as though the bouquet were
stinking fish. Or perhaps, gripped in mid-stem, he totes
it like luggage. Or with feigned disdain shoves it roughly
into a backpack from which one or two blossoms gaily nod,
proclaiming to all the wide-eyed, snickering world, *Here is a
fool, here is a fool for love.*

Seasons

Certainly there are more than four. Breton says fifteen or so.
Arp says it's winter every Monday. The Inuit say there are
six, including those that contain the small material for winter
and for spring. When you look at me as you do now, that is a
season. That look contains the small material for joy, another
season that comes and goes unpredictably throughout the year.
I hope when I die it will be in a season of joy and that you will
circle the date on a calendar as having been the longest day.

Skipping

Tick. Tick. Tick. Tick. All in together girls it's fine weather girls when is your birthday please jump in. Tick. Tick. Tick. Each tick is a frame, the frame of a jump, a snippet of the movie of a girl skipping. There is a jump in coordination when such skills are acquired and what was once impossible, frustrating, infuriating becomes proud-easy. She goes fast, faster, how many frames per second, the blur as the rope circles and the girl within its arc is inside a time machine, moving into the future. With each revolution, the second-hand rope ticks away her childhood. You almost want her to miss just once, to pull her back to the present, so afraid are you that she will skip right out of your life and leave you here flat-footed on this earth.

At the End of the Street

You walk the dog round the corner and come face-to-face with a luminous harvest moon, closer than you have ever seen her before. How kindly this feels, as though a socially-prominent relative had finally deigned to visit your rundown part of town — and wearing the gown of the season at that! How wonderfully warm! You want to come nearer; a few more steps and you could kiss her cheek. But the dog is sniffing here and there, pulling the leash in other directions, and the golden girl starts to raise herself from the scruffy street and put on airs again. You hurry the dog through her business and run home for your moon-eyed wife and daughter. But the two of them, madonna and child, have fallen asleep and will not wake. By the time you return, alone, she's back in her unapproachable sky. She is everyone's again, distant and untouchable as any Hollywood star. Only her gown is a little shadowed at one edge where the queen of heaven knelt for a moment at the end of your dirty street.

Creatures

The dried up fly
on the sill between the panes
is my birthstone.
    — Stan Rice

Big Cat Circus

We instantly conjure snarling lions and tigers. A hairy-chested
Tarzan with his head between fierce jaws. A ring of fire, a
whip and chair, a man with a pistol outside the cage in case.
So how surprised, and, at first, disappointed we are when the
lights go up to see the man with the chair sitting in it, too
frail to stand. An old gent in bedroom slippers, with a huge
fat tabby in his lap. For a long while, the fur ball does nothing,
only blinks and purrs. Then finally, action! The geezer lifts
the great weight from his knees — the first feat of the night —
and deposits the creature in front of a saucer of milk. The cat
makes the milk disappear — domesticated magic! His trainer's
pride seems hardly circus-scale: at best, a shy smile. He pulls
from his pocket a squirming mouse, which he dangles by the
tail. No sooner have its feet touched ground than the wide cat
swipes out a paw and pins it alive. For the next few minutes,
the mouse is caught and released till all but we die-hard lovers
of spectacle have filed out. The drum-roll finale comes when
granddad pries open the none-too-deadly jaws and slips a
milky finger inside the cat's mouth, feeding him the last drop.
A barely audible meow signals the end. The old man stuffs the
pudge in his travelling case, and shuffles out of the spotlight,
leaving the chair. But oh, what melancholy descends upon the
faithful when the romance of sawdust and tinsel leaves town
and moves on!

Meow

She's losing her hearing, her vision, her balance and her
marbles. She's into her third decade — old for a cat. She
who had kept her own counsel, aloof all her life, has begun
speaking and crying, accusingly, at all hours, and her voice has
developed an unsettling plaintive intensity.

When they leave the house, she's convinced they will
never return, and begins croaking a pitiable "Hello?" When
they turn off the lights and go to bed, she cries out "Help!
Help! Help!" as if they have shut her in a small dark room,
straitjacketed, in a wheelchair. These are no anthropomorphic
projections. The subtlety and range of her articulation
has clearly improved with need. Her vocal powers now
demonstrate the sophistication of so-called primitive peoples,
taking on the intense and strange musicality of Innu throat
singers, the childlike singsong of the Cameroon pygmy. Like
Tibetan monks who attain nirvana chanting, she has mastered
the art of two notes at once. The colour and quality of her
howling is more various than they would have thought
possible, possessed of a vibrato rich with expressive quavers
and demi-quavers. And the artful repetitions, without pause,
suggest she has mastered the complex circular breathing of the
aboriginal players of the didgeridoo.

In her desperate isolation, she's become the senile old
mother neither of them has, and she goads them with
uncharacteristic cursing. She cries like it is a question: "Oh,
hell! Oh, hell!" The throatiness that would have been pleasant
in a happy, purring animal is downright sinister in this fur-
and-bone wraith who haunts the house with such restlessness.
"Oooooh, ooooh, ooooh!" No amount of food sates her,

no amount of door opening makes her feel either free or welcome. Whichever side she's on is the wrong one; they wait for her to die.

At least he does. She is the wife's, and perhaps he has the lesser portion of sympathy. But if they argue over the right thing to do, they are judged by cries of "Row! Row!" down the darkened hall, and once, in a computer-like monotone, the horrible verdict "Error!" If, exasperated, they — he — should shout at her to shut the hell up, she answers with a plaintive "Me? Owwww!," as if she were in excruciating pain and he the most unsympathetic of sons-in-law.

Naturally, they take her to the vet. Not wanting to appear heartless, they can't say they are going mad, that their beloved pet has taken on the character of Poe's tell-tale heart, nagging them incessantly over all the wrongs they've done to every sensate being in creation. Tactfully they suggest that perhaps she's in pain, hoping if such could be proven they would have a case for putting her down. The vet, a relentlessly cheerful young woman whose elderly mother runs marathons and edits a seniors' newsletter called *Grey Power*, assures them after minute examination that she is, for her advanced age, surprisingly well, and advises them to *enjoy her while you still can*. Her tone says it is they who have been weighed and found bloodless, they who are wanting, they who are wrong, immoral, ungrateful children who would pitch their own mother into a home, hissing and scratching, at the first sign of impairment, or smother her with a pillow while she slept in the in-law suite. So they stand condemned. Having chosen animal life, they must now accept the full experience, including the unanticipated transformation of pet to master, which accompanies the slow descent to death.

Nocturnal Visitors

They're not fooling anyone with those Lone Ranger masks, a disguise as thin as Clark Kent's glasses. But they're super with their hands — opening garbage cans, unwrapping fish guts — believe me, you don't know the half. They climbed down our tree one night while we finished our drinks. My watch was drying on the picnic table after it had slipped off into the punch. The mother took it apart in the dark and licked its gears clean while her kits tied my shoelaces together. It keeps better time now than it ever did — a bit slow in the day, but always sharp at night. It's only the nine-to-five that keeps them out of dentistry and the bomb squad. With the right piano, Chopin would be a breeze.

Coyote on the Avenue

You're the one they post signs about in the park. Little do they
know how often you make like Geronimo in *Stagecoach* and
"jump the reservation." At the intersection of our midnight
rambles, the wild and the domestic transgress their boundaries.
Our eyes meet, co-conspirators, and seem to say Don't tell.

Dog

We reckon her every year as seven-multiplied. But imagine
then her days, her minutes, hours she has spent this morning
sniffing pee. What were her seven or seven hundred thoughts?
If she has sailed one sea, seen one wonder, she has sailed and
seen them all. Consider, in her prime, her sevenfold orgasms.
Should she and I die today in a Sabbath car crash, she will
have outlived me, savoured and suffered more. At our deaths,
it will be only right that she be grieved seven times longer,
that seven mates and seventy-seven children should howl
through seven lean years at seven moons.

Mouse

He steals out every night when things fall quiet, scurrying
down the hallway into the kitchen. By the time the shadow
he is registers in the brain, it's too late to take off a slipper and
hurl it. We've tried spring traps, glue traps, even poison. Still
he reappears, a modest domestic version of the apocalyptic
plagues on the late news. He pokes his head round the corner,
stares balefully at us, before vanishing into an air vent. For a
while, he holed up beneath the oven, and we half expected
him to pop up through the centre of the stovetop, our own
private Whack-a-Mole, taunting us to clobber him. One night
you dreamed I was hammering at my old typewriter, cursing
the relic for gaps it left in the text. Turned out every time
I struck certain letters, it hit the sleeping mouse on the head,
till the poor thing was stupefied and halfway dead. And of
course it's true that MOUSE is in the keys of my typewriter.
Also CAT, who you'd think might solve our problem; even
ELEPHANT, who is imposing, but afraid of mice. And this
dream brings back a joke I heard as a child, about a man too
poor to buy bait for his mousetrap, and uses instead a picture
of a piece of cheese. What he caught is what I've caught by
typing this.

Butterflies

On the overgrown garden path, they flutter up into a startling banner headline, the marks on each wing resembling letters of the alphabet. This message was just for me, but I wasn't wearing my glasses. I hoped there might be an evening edition that I could peruse at leisure.

Bats

Like feeding seagulls, you toss things into the air to lure them
in. How disappointing, these pebbles and shards of bark. Still,
they come lower and lower till they're practically eating from
your hand, and old wives shriek at the prospect of getting
them caught in their hair. Tale though it is, and nothing to
fear, that drunken swoop, the tilted flopping flight convinces
us they're crazy: blind drivers on the 401, dark mayhem.

Bat, Mistaken

Why this dump of soggy tea leaves in the sink? Trying to read my fortune? Misapprehension — unless the future is crumpled leather wings and little hooks, a shadow of doubt that comes at night and shakes the falsely-reassuring green light of the carbon monoxide monitor. Dark clot on white curtains, it hung by tiny feet while I hunted the empty tea canister. But when I turned my back, it flapped another tipsy circuit round the room and dropped behind a punched-tin candleholder, where its black spark would not be blown out, eternal flame.

Next evening at dusk, we watched rags of winged night seep from cracks in the attic and drop-launch themselves into the tea-coloured future. They wobbled off, catching in that dim light things we couldn't make out. Their squeaks of echolocation were rusty hinges on a door to another world.

Lost: Shadow

he is lost and grey and might land on my shoulder but they
say I must not be frightened he probably won't bite what will
it be like to have shadow fall on me at noon or midnight in a
poorly lit alley is he small as he appears in his wanted poster
or does fear make him loom larger can I be patient remain
calm will his silent swoop not take me by surprise and his
sudden copper talons grabbing my shoulder from above not
startle me to yell which will unbalance poor shadow into
biting just to hang on

   or will he be gentle with me is he as lonely as I am o lost
shadow please find your caged and shady brother I will not
renounce you despite the promise of reward I will move
through my days with someone else's shadow on my shoulder
light as feathers the dark friend I never had whispering pirated
wisdom into my ear

Firefly

In your jar, you are my faint-hope lantern, frail guide through
the night by my bed. On a shelf in the pitch-black cottage
you circle a tiny kingdom — a miniature lighthouse sweeping
the coastline of solitude. As I drift off, you keep vigil. Your
ember fails and flares, the fiery end of a smoke as a father
watches over his sleeping son, thinking his dark private
thoughts.

Fables

I say we ought to go back
to cars pulled by horses
to steam-driven planes
to TV sets cut from stone.
    — *Nicanor Parra*

Drought

The wells in our town yield only buckets of sand. Last year,
I joined my father to dig another. We dug deeper than ever
before. There were three fights, and one man was killed with a
shovel before we gave up. Walking to school, my little brother
asks if it's cooler down in the well. I tell him no, in fact it's
stifling hot. There's no breeze down there, and the dry walls
close in on your shoulders. Besides, you're getting steadily closer
to Hell. Before school starts, we are scratching with sticks in the
dirt, drawing pictures of naked girls with jugs like watermelons...

In school they teach about people who live beside oceans. At
first I envied those wise and fortunate tribes. But father says they
are fools who drink their own piss. I advise my brother to colour
his oceans black.

A road once led out of town toward a beautiful lake. Or so
they say. It must have been years ago. Wind and dust have long
since erased any track in whichever direction. Those curious few
who set out to find it never returned.

Sometimes in the evenings the elders recall the old days.
They speak of a dragon-shaped river, talk fondly of floods. Their
stories flow on in a slow meandering far into the night, and
though the truth of their words is murky, they sound sweet and
trickle into my dreams.

My granddad is one of those who remember rain. He says he
once saw it fall for a week without stopping. At the thought his
voice quavers, and his gnarled fingers stiffen like thirsty roots.
For a moment I imagine him young, his eyes clear and green,
with strength and vigour flowing through his limbs. Cataracts
cloud his vision now; he will never see rain again. He falls back
into his chair, a dried-up husk of a man. A breath, a sigh, seems
to empty him, but he does not, or cannot, cry.

Batman Pushing Sixty

I was never super anyway — the paunch should be no
surprise. Besides, tights don't flatter anyone at this age. After
Robin tested positive, I went into a tailspin, pissed away the
Wayne fortune, lost the mansion and car to loan sharks. I drank
myself out of shape. Muggers laughed when I'd swoop down
and twist an ankle on landing. Got pistol-whipped once, had
to crawl to Emerg like a cottage bat swatted with a tennis
racquet. That's when I retired for good. Now the Dark Knight
calculates risk for Sun Life insurance. A comedown, but what
can you do? Even Superman's no hero since a Kryptonite
fragment rendered him virtually powerless. They say all he has
left is heat vision, which he uses to make tea and toast as he
sits with his clippings, forgotten in that Fortress-of-Solitude
seniors' home.

School Days

For forgetfulness, the teacher keeps you after school to clean
the boards. You obliterate acres of knowledge in classrooms
up and down the hall — history, science, geometry, the
conjugation of the verb *to be*. You may never *be* again, at
least not correctly. Schools ought to make you smart,
but you feel stupider than ever, having wiped out whole
continents, centuries. The Dewey digestive system, Einstein's
Theory of Cousins and Uncles, the War between Synonyms
and Antonyms — dim memories. School is once more a
blank slate, the proofs lost in a mushroom chalk-cloud of
unknowing. On the primal playground, the clapping of
erasers is applause for ignorance. In a frenzy of anti-learning,
you start burning books.

Red River

Was The West always so hollow, Monument Valley echoing
like an empty airplane hangar, John Ford on his hands and
knees trying to reassemble the wreckage? Civilization all false
fronts, breakaway bar stools and sugar glass, John Wayne the
macho disguise of a man named Marion. When my father
spoke of his Tiger Hills, I thought he was seeing Arcadia, so
clear was the far-off yearning in his eyes. In the scrub along
our Red River, I was explorer, trailblazer…now only gas-
guzzling SUVs. Under threat of arrest, the outlaw Neruda
escapes on horseback through a mountain pass into Argentina.
What poetry's left since red ants carried his last tiny grains
into secret caves deep under the Andes?

Stick-Horse John Wayne

In *The Searchers'* lost original print, John Wayne rides a stick
horse and shoots with his finger, BAM! Texas is a vacant lot
down the lane from Ward Bond's house, and the homestead a
crude rectangle of fallen leaves with door- and window-gaps.
The kidnapped Natalie Wood is another knee-scraped nine-
year-old whose incessant between-takes kissing of 'Indians'
stokes the Duke's nascent racism. With so few props to prop
him up, he can barely swagger through the leaf doors without
wrecking them, a bull in the china shop of civilized emotion.
Yet for one held moment they're still innocent, improvising,
the script for their tragedy not yet fixed. So John Ford sets

up a lemonade stand and sells drinks at 5¢ a glass for forty
years, till he can manage real horses, real guns and slightly less
phony Indians. BAM! BAM! Now Wayne growls *That'll be the
day!* with his full weight of intransigence. We watch him shoot
out the eyes of the dead Comanch, and wonder who's truly
doomed *to wander forever between the winds.*

I Saw Nana Mouskouri Naked

A shouldered sack, though it was New Year's, not Christmas, Eve. His worldly goods, and a hand-lettered sign round his neck. Surely it would read *No home, no job, please help*. But no: *Respectful to Archangel Michael and all other Holy Angels*. We stood respectful together at the WAIT TO CROSS gate of tomorrow, a moment of looking forward, looking back. My looking was broken: two pair bust in two days, the old ones held together with scratchy tape. There seemed no hope for vision. Opticians would see no one, their eyes darkened early; the library had already closed its books on the year. Off-duty librarian angels stared anxiously into New Year's traffic with the rest of us. Only Pandemonium — all demons — still beckoned: used books and music — SALE.

I grovelled on the lower shelves, hoping for poetry. In one hand, *Twenty Love Poems and a Song of Despair*; in the other, *Play the Piano Drunk Like a Percussion Instrument Until the Fingers Begin to Bleed a Bit*. In he came to hawk his CDs, each preciously wrapped in a story. I didn't look up. In one fairy tale, a foreign guitarist needed direction to the concert hall, and repaid him with tickets and a peep backstage. *And that's when I saw Nana Mouskouri naked*. The bargains of love and despair, of my bleeding fingers — I shut my eyes and joined him in his respectful reverie: an angel revealed, the body and visage shining. *Not bad looking*, he said, *except for those god-awful glasses!*

Her Parents Did Not Approve

As if passing on a friend's obit, Mother reports the most
beautiful girl in my class up and married a clown. *But not
a happy clown*, she says, shaking her head. *He had only one
name.* Did she take his name? I wonder. Are they sleeping in
the gutter, two born-to-the-spotlight headliners huddled now
under a single name, braving bitter Winnipeg winters, their
makeup streaked, with nothing to laugh at the rest of their
emaciated lives?

Propitiation

In the dark barn I squirm on my farm-boy father's open palm, my Isaac tail held tight between Abraham fingers. We have no vision, only faith in the sudden rush of air as the shadow lord of the loft descends in silence and blesses us with the rough touch of talons. Each in our time, we are spirited away to his high dark corner where he reduces us to a scat of hair and indigestible bones.

Wrong House

What are we doing here? Mother cries, in deep and obvious distress. *This isn't our house! Get me out of here!* Her daughter winces, as though stabbed with a pickle fork. *There's your bedroom,* she says patiently, *there's the photo of Papa. Of course this is your house. Whose house would it be?* The napkin Mother has shredded since lunch is a breadcrumb trail meandering behind her, room to unfamiliar room.

Not ours, not ours, mutters Mother, as she moves now to tearing at the buttons of her dress, worrying the rings round her fingers. Finally her daughter decides there is nothing else for it. *Okay, Mother, you win. We're leaving. I'll drive you back to our place.* And bundled into the car, the old woman gazes like a newborn at the wide world rolling by as they troll slowly round the block. It's like a trip through time, through decades and several cities. And when they drive up to the same house again, for the third time that day, her daughter sings out *Well, here we are!* and the old woman is delighted too. *At last,* she says, *I was beginning to think I'd never see home again!*

The Man With Nine Thousand Names

When his wife calls him to supper, does he answer? Or has he truly
forgotten his own first name? He's down-cellar — urban sprawl of
scrawl — where his obsession is out of hand. From his excess of
identity, he is pruning the spare, the unwanted, the illegible sloppy
seconds, the nicked names. But only to buy new ones, or trade
up for finer samples: rare names, lost names with foreign accents,
the Biblical, the antique, the *noms de plumes* and stage names, the
criminal aliases, names he's never pronounced or even heard before.
Sign your John Henry, your John Hancock, your John Doe. He will
swap his unloved names for yours.

You hesitate: *My father gave me this. It's all I have. I probably
shouldn't part with it.* But he admires it, flattering, persistent. Pick
any name you like, says the honeyed voice. An entire small-town
phone book lies before you, manifold personalities. Beautiful, sad
or silly, Christian or patronymic, names of the living and the dead,
titled names, pet names, names in unfamiliar alphabets, names
with many consonants, names with only a few. Names of the justly
famous, and the humble names they were born with. Names shared
with murderers, later changed in shame. Names to confound spell-
checkers, names to horrify the officers of restricted clubs. With such
names you could be spoken of for generations.

He offers bargains: hyphenated names two-for-one, discounts
on maiden names, the gender-neutral, the rhyming names of twins,
surnames with ambiguous initials. Why not give him your unknown,
forgettable name? Your father will never know. Your wife can still
whisper it in your ear. Mail it along, imagine it issuing through the
slot, welcomed like sunshine. It lies openly on the page, not crabbed
and inscrutable. Taking your good name, this Adam-in-reverse will
smile. Your future fame — or infamy — is his to hoard now for as
long as he takes breath.

Identity

Your late mother holds you as a baby in her arms. She's wearing a print dress and a plastic belt with a large buckle, standing before a rough house whose chimney is leaning precariously. You tell everyone this is the only surviving picture of the two of you, that it came to light on your uncle's recent death, in a box of things he rescued from the fire and never had the heart to sort out.

You have it enlarged and framed. It is then you notice for the first time a cigarette between the fingers of her left hand. Odd, because your mother never smoked. And the baby looks surprisingly fair, while you and your parents were dark.

You stare at the picture often, and are doing so one day when the phone rings. A woman's voice says your name as a question, and when you say Yes? she says it doesn't sound like you. Well, it *is* me, you say, annoyed; who else would it be? And as though speaking through a tin can down a long string, she says again, it doesn't sound like you.

Outgoing

Sorry I can't come to the phone just now. I shipped out this
morning on a slip of soap, sailing across the bathroom floor
and cracking my skull on the sink. Since then I've been lying
on the deck unable to move, wondering where I'm bound and
how long before I see land again. The journey has not been
unpleasant, save for the headache and the lack of food and
drink. Still, I've done nothing to exert myself, so my
needs are few. Since I perform no duties, it would appear
I'm a passenger and not a member of the crew; they've
left me entirely alone to work on my tan and revise in my
throbbing head this message I didn't have time to record.
I spent the daylight hours in a reverie, listening to the cries
of seabirds, the creaking of the ropes and the slap of sails as
they bellied out in the wind. Now night has fallen, it's grown
chill, and I don't recognize the constellations, which makes
me think perhaps we've entered the southern hemisphere. I'm
pretending to teach myself celestial navigation, but the truth
is I have no idea of our course or destination, or even the
purpose of my journey, if indeed I had one. For this reason,
I can't promise if or when I'll return your call, but I thank you
again for phoning. I wish you Godspeed.

Child's Hand

Horrified at their find, they immediately rope off the beach. What greater omen of depravity than this tiny hand severed from its body? They will sift sand for clues from now till doomsday; the saw-toothed sin lies somewhere, and they vow to name it. But wait. Days later they announce their mistake: the hand is a doll's hand. And everyone wonders what fools are these experts in crime that cannot tell child from doll, butchery from carelessness. How striking that cops and doctors could be so badly beaten, so fiercely and fearfully gripped by such a tiny hand. How could they hold it without noticing that its blood was their own bloody-mindedness? What darkness was in them that they should assume evil before innocence, attach *foul* to all play? Or are there somewhere dolls so perfectly child-like that parents and toymakers can't tell them apart? Perhaps wind and water *do* age plastic to flesh — perverse alchemy — the hand's tiny lifeline realistically short, the pink baby fat weathered a sandy grey. On the shore, a body is Christ-broken for scavenger gulls, whose stuck-record cries pass for the bleat of lost lambs.

Left for Right

When he offered, it felt right, save for the underhanded
thumb. He was very artful. A hand like his might have
palmed a one-eyed jack, lifted a wallet, or switched,
unnoticed, a pretty assistant's mole to her opposite cheek.
After shaking hands, I wanted to count my fingers. Now
I can't stop watching that single dexterous hand adapt like
the flounder, whose eyes migrate as needed from one side to
the other. Driving, buttoning, cinching things…all effortless
tricks for the old hand moving mirror-smooth through the
dominant, one-sided world — ambiguous, almost right, but
somehow sinister.

Too Tight

A teenage boy suddenly dies, and his mother is devastated. She weeps uncontrollably day after day, barely able to put one foot in front of the other. His body is laid to rest, but night after night he appears to his mother in dreams. The priest promises another mass in forty days, to rest his spirit. The mother is unconsoled. This is no fleeting apparition that will fade over forty days. Since his death, he hobbles to her every night complaining his shoes are too tight.

The mother seeks out her grandmother, now past ninety, who married at sixteen and has outlived three of her children. How should she help her poor beautiful boy who has died too young in tight shoes? A child's death is a punishment no one deserves, to which has now been added this guilt: that she failed to properly clothe him. Can Grandmother offer some advice? How does one help a dead boy who can't rest for the ache in his growing feet?

Buy him bigger shoes, says the old woman. The tormented mother wails. Must she now be afflicted with a crazy grandmother too? How will he wear them? she protests. It doesn't matter, says Grandmother. Give them to another boy, someone his age, whose feet they will fit. So the mother buys shoes, good ones, a size bigger than those he was buried in, and the pinch of this unfitting death eases a little for them all.

Fox and Not-Fox

Every year our country celebrates the legend of Fox. There are paintings of Fox, books about Fox, vacant cartoon pictures of Fox for children to fill with bright colour. In a movie, an actor pretends to be Fox; he smiles like Fox, waves like Fox, runs like Fox, re-enacting the tale of his epic journey. Today they have told my daughter the legend of Fox, how he fell into the trap of suffering and lost a leg in its jaws. How he saw a vision of the end of suffering and called upon the gods to make it so. How he limped to the edge of the eastern ocean, and with great ceremony dipped in his lost leg and set himself the heroic task, saying, *I will run across the land, across the rocky ground and the swamp, through the forests and over the prairies and the mountains to the western ocean so that the gods will be moved, their stony hearts broken with pity. No one else will lose a leg as I have: I will not stop until the gods promise me this.*

His followers led him. They lured him with the scent of food, with the promise of rest, with sympathy for his loss. Fox ran after them all day, every day, hopping on his lost leg, and at evening he went to ground. At first no one saw him, he was not noticed, he was only a tiny figure in a great wide land hopping alongside its ditches and up its hills. But the longer he ran, the more others came to know of him. He came to them in their dreamtime, on their cave walls. As he ran, faster travellers recognized him by his wild hair and the hitch in his gait as he hopped. They made noises to cheer him on, they yelled and waved and smiled. Charity overtook them and they threw coins. They heard of his vow and wanted to help. They would be home first, they would be home long before him, but Fox didn't care. Fox ran on. He was young and strong, he could run through rain, through fog and sun and snow. He missed his leg, he was hurting where his leg used to be, his lost leg became larger and larger, became powerful, became mythic. He was in pain but he ran on, pursuing and pursued. He was running west toward the setting sun.

Finally the unseen seized him. He had glimpsed it out of the corner of his eye, in the swamps, in the shadows at dusk. He had heard it in the howl of the wind, felt it in the bite of the snow. All along it had been with him, hidden like a secret inside him. It had been with him every step of the way, stealing his blood, stealing his breath, stealing the food from his mouth. While he ran west, it ran too, stronger than he, never sleeping. It sat now on his chest in the night and said *I have beaten you, you cannot outrun me. No*, said Fox, *I am not beaten.* But the next day, Fox told his followers to carry him home. People everywhere heard him weeping, people everywhere tasted the salt of his tears in their daily bread. People ached in their bones for Fox, sorrowed in their hearts for Fox; with every breath, people whispered his name. When Fox reached home, the people called him Hero. When he died, they vowed never to forget him.

When she learns the legend of Fox, my daughter runs round a field in his name. He was not a quitter, she says. Her teachers use him as a lesson, to prod the children forward, a gold coin nailed to the masthead, a selfless character in a morality play. He runs in bronze forever now on his *via dolorosa*. He will never die again. His martyrdom is perfect.

They do not teach her about Not-Fox, who followed the trail of Fox and did not die. He too lost a leg, and ran and ran. He ran through rain and wind, over prairies and mountains, and reached the western ocean. But he has no legend of his own. His achievement is whispered away, a poor shadow. No one runs in his name. There is no celebration in his honour. He has no followers, he has not done the heroic thing and died. He too was young, and squandered the legacy of love that might have been extended to one who followed in the footsteps of Fox.

Not-Fox is forgotten; children do not praise him from sea to sea. He is the dark runner, surly, unfavoured and unloved. He is The One Who Came After, patron saint of jealous brothers, of footnotes. He ran to the ocean, yet to this day, there are those who do not believe, who claim he was merely carried on the strong back of Fox. In the shadow of Fox, the Hero and the legend, Not-fox lives anxiously, without direction. For now he is no one, nothing; the gods have turned him back into a man.

Things

I do love to compare apples with oranges.
— *Lyn Hejinian*

Bookmarks

Slipping into a new high bed, we tuck fresh pages under our chins and dream novel dreams. At first the blankets are few, but as the nights progress there are more and more. At the equinox, the thickness above is as great as the one below, but from then on the mattress grows thinner and the weight of bedclothes more crushing. The sad fact is we cannot control the quality of our sleep. The book they can't put down is *our* insomnia. If the reader bolts on the second page at the honk of the airport cab, we may spend weeks shivering under the thin sheet of page one. But the lost book is the worst, an accident resulting in vegetative coma. Imagine dreaming the same unresolved fragment of a dream, over and over in endless night, for the rest of your long flat life!

Peculiar Book

In FLYSPECK BOOKS, its cover looked vaguely familiar — a
Rorschach of blurred figures, perhaps a love triangle. Back
home in my favourite wingback, I thought to read it in a
single sitting. But now as the tale unfolds, the typeface seems
shrunken. Thick rectos and versos thumb apart into multiple
onionskin pages. The simple story grows labyrinthine, full
of subplots and secret identities. The jacket, on closer study,
bears no illustration at all, only the soil of grubby fingers and
a stain that might be blood. I glance toward the clock, but
my eyes no longer focus, not at any distance. Snared in the
book's looping timeline, I'm no longer certain what day it is.
When I entered the house of this book, I expected sunlight in
the few rooms and delicate portraits in which I would notice
some family resemblance. Instead there are ghosts, endless
passageways and lock after lock. With my eye to the next
keyhole, I can make out only shadows, though a weeping that
sounds familiar is coming from the other side of the door.

Bar of Soap

She loves handmade soap. Every few weeks a new brick
appears, neatly cut like fudge or igloo snow. Boastfully
all natural, and fragrant with lavender, honey or vanilla.
Sometimes they're opaque and rough with leaf bits or seed;
other times they're candy-smooth and the light shines through.
In the shower this morning my blind reach found an amber
one; embedded in the centre, a dark shape that might have
had wings. As I washed, I imagined it fluttered. Passing it over
my face, my genitals, I hesitated.

Corner Store

Weekend mornings in the quiet, he reads the gospels by the cash. It's a miracle stale loaves and tinned fishes fill so many. But it's mostly *smoke* and curved mirrors, lotto tickets, junk food, skin books. He has two Christian names, an English one and his real one. He works ungodly hours so his kids don't have to; they live in a shoebox upstairs. His wife hasn't learned to smile, though she did cut her hair, which makes her look brighter. She's sour like the milk. Why should Lucky Convenience be so inconvenient, so unlucky? Unlucky at being robbed, unlucky her English is broken, unlucky at being pinched for selling *smoke* to minors. In her own defence, she starts a petition asking customers to vouch for her, but it's too late; she's already been cornered.

Chair for Rent

Consider: what more do you really need? One chair is all
most men can handle. It's comfortable, upholstered in leather,
swivels and tilts at a touch. True, it can't be moved, is in
fact bolted to the floor, but the company is pleasant and the
conversation can be stimulating or restrained depending on
your preference. The rent is so reasonable you could, if you
chose, simply sit there each afternoon staring at the ceiling,
dozing off to Verdi or the ball game. Or, if you care to, you
could engage in a sort of sublet while you get up and walk
around, making snipping motions, telling jokes to your
captive audience.

Bubble Gum

From masticated lumps, he fashions portraits. Mostly teen idols, whose bubble gum music's dismissed. He doesn't do all the chewing. School kids can be bought with candy. Brittany's hair, her lips, her eyes, all mouth-made, at recess. Celebrity calls for so many unnatural colours. A girl called Brittany probably chewed Brittany's face — some of it, anyway. Spit it out, Brittany. What colours best capture the sugary soul of two Brittanys, each with that same cow-chewing-cud expression? Will a week's detention make a star? Was it worth it? Each pop face sells for much more than a pack of gum, but then art is more nourishing, isn't it?

Balloon Tires

They call it a beach bike. Next to the Italian racing models, or even your old ten-speed, this looks like something designed by Botero. No thoroughbred filly, more like a dancing hippo, the water horse. No g-string saddle, no tightrope tires, no handlebars curlicue-twisted into ram's horns, this is transport for those in no hurry to get anywhere. The cyclist will not hunch over, transforming into some aerodynamic teardrop, encased in spandex and crash helmet as though ready to be shot from a cannon. No, the rider of this contraption sits erect, gazes casually side to side and may well be wearing baggy pants with clips and a Panama hat. The seat belongs on a tractor, its pudgy rubber cushioning the jarring impact of potholes. The handlebars are a graceful insouciant moustache from another era.

Indeed, the whole thing is a throwback to a time when motion was not a blur, when bicycles scarcely moved faster than strolling men. Before pencil-necked geeks with slide rules calculated gear ratios of peddled energy to motive power; before fenders were stripped away as so much dead weight; before speed became an addiction and the bicycle, like the rider's body, became the alloyed, crafted, competitive weapon of the modern Tour de France. The love of speed may be fast, but the speed of love is slow. This is the vehicle of courtship, of leisure and pleasure, of picnic baskets and June swoon tunes. Tell Spielberg the ones in *ET* are all wrong. If ever a bicycle might float cross the face of the moon, this one, with its fat balloon tires, is surely it.

Lake

Adrift in a peapod. Nothing more perfect than to relinquish
control on the molten glass of this dark lake, trailing a hand
in the softness, listening to the trill it makes, watching the
heron — intent, scholarly — practicing his art of patience.
Look down and behold a watery reading room with countless
Art Nouveau lamps, their slender green necks curving up
from shadowy depths, culminating in white blossom shades.
Above them, the drifting skylight of my yellow canoe and a
purposeful white gull, an idea heading somewhere.

A Stone

All stones are broken stones, but this one's more than just broken. Agglomerate, unevenly worn, hard planes dividing irregular spaces, a drunken honeycomb. A Gaudi block in miniature, with tiny stone balconies and privacy fences, and no two apartments alike. Never a SUITE FOR RENT sign — must be a waiting list to live here. Its architectural scale being so different from our own, it follows that other scales must likewise be different. Can't begin to guess, for example, what rents might be. We've been watching, through twelve years of nightfall, for lights to go on in the tiny rooms, and for curious faces to look out, trying to gauge tomorrow's weather.

Death of the Life of the Party

She suddenly toppled and lay there with limbs quite still.
Once quivery and sensitive, she seemed now wooden, smaller
than before and undeniably naked. But we took her in,
spangled and baubled her up, and made her the life of the
party. She sucked back all she could drink as if there was no
tomorrow. Then, like a leper, she began dropping herself all
over. There seemed no cure for the illness slowly turning her
brown, and finally, after New Year's, we agreed her day was
past. With little ceremony, we gave up her body to the flames.
In hindsight, we should have seen a bad end coming when
the axe first appeared. As to what to do with her tell-tale foot,
sticking accusingly out of the earth, we're truly stumped.

73

The Rink

In blades so old they might have belonged to the '29 Leafs,
I step on the snow-covered lake to clear off a rink. My
child and I will skate here, perform graceful arabesques and
pirouettes, shoot amazing goals, fly down the wings and
stop in a shower of stars. We'll break for hot chocolate, then,
ploughing fresh paths with the shovel, glide in meandering
trade routes as far as we care to travel. A god-like freedom,
to walk on water, skating rings round the islands, up and
down channels, through the marsh where, in summer, the
heron observes his prey on his long skinny legs, the sceptical
professor with his question mark neck. And indeed, the lake
has a surprise in store — beneath the skiff of snow, not ice but
living water. I sink, and find myself skating along the bottom,
visible to my astonished family only as the scoop of the high-
held shovel breaking the far horizon like the topmost, wind-
bellied sail of the Flying Dutchman.

Slush

It's like walking through applesauce, the clean crisp white,
once so sharp and exhilarating, gone brown, sad and
mushy. The sloppy seconds of a season known for its cold
ruthless heart, its graves like iron, its bitter winds, its black
ice. Corners are the worst: little elbow lakes. You attempt
an awkward, indecisive half-jump stride and come down
soaking your shoes, splashing your pants. Maybe twist your
ankle, slip, fall, make yourself a wet fool, join the senile drool
and dribble of Old Man Winter. Spattered by heedless cars,
shoes taking on water like a sinking ship, you schlep yourself
home bedraggled, hobbled, sodden, pathetic. Can climate
age us, alter our character? Here is the proof: one way to be
weathered.

Buried Sky

They're replacing the pipes in my neighbourhood. What a shock — the new ones are beautiful blue! Not industrial black or grey, but a flamboyant Broadway blue, a true blue that no one will ever see, pure as summer sky. People will walk these streets the rest of their lives blind to the network of sky-blue tubes that supports their flushing and bathing and drinking. They'll walk dusty streets, snowy streets, muddy streets under monotonous grey skies never knowing that tubular blue sky lies buried beneath their feet. But I will be haunted by this knowledge. And lying on my back looking up at heaven, I'll think of that other blue sky lying on its back, looking up at the earth.

Our Sister

Fontanelle was clearly soft in the head when he claimed he could tell from here what your people were like — burned black by the sun, he said, and full of fire, always in love and occupied daily with verse. All this he inferred from your radiance morning and night. We know better now. You are hostile to life itself, let alone poetry. You are dry, of volcanic temperament, all your nights moonless. Named for beauty, your face is pockmarked and cratered. Some christen you Lucy — for Lucifer — behind your back. You sulk under boiling cloud, your own drama-queen world of constant thunderstorm. Calling you sister was a mistake. You spin your own way, opposite to the rest of us.

77

Soap Bubbles

Blown free, they spin on various axes, random planets governed by different suns. In each, swirling gold and blue clouds move over the face of the deep: breathtaking weather. Some are speared instantly on wild rice and marsh grass. Others tumble over the still waters of the channel, our tiny selves growing ever smaller within them. A few seem half-absorbed dockside. We look down into them as into many crystal balls, as though a dozen psychics had predicted that our future would include precisely this moment, and released us into the cosmic wind to meet it. On the curved surface, there is a moment of trembling, a gold swirl in which we are small figures on a horizon of dockwood. Then clouds of blue sweep over us in a shudder and we see our last moment flash golden again, sheet lightning across the dome of a tiny heaven, before we pop like Christmas lights: brief beauty, a glimpse of something, a life winking out.

Wool

row on row it grows the shawl knitted by all the patient
women needing needles or imaging imagine what those hands
need they need to fidget while they fret so someone stocks
the waiting rooms with waiting wool & knitting needles &
women needing needles or imagining images of tumours
fidget a lumpy scarf as long as their waiting & if they drop
a stitch when their name is NEXT that stitch is picked up
by the next waiting one who carries on as women do & so
the shawl sweater scarf blanket grows & grows a counter-
cancer of comfort under watchful eyes of worried women the
implacable clacking of needles women come & go occupying
the same few seats all morning & afternoon a succession
of counter-LaFarges knitting the shadow of death into a
healthwork of waiting a womanwarmth of together sweaters
arm-in-arm scarves one-for-all shawls to wrap round the
shaking shoulders of whomever receives the bad call a shawl
to warm that wounded woman whose news says she will lose
a breast the ball of waiting wool is a skein of fidgeted fate an
ongoing knitting of women together in need & compassion a
way to say to each other I care I understand I sat here like you
I fidgeted too & feared what they would find & as I go off to
the desperate room of truth I leave this ravelled sleeve of care
for you to carry on may it say to you have faith keep warm
wrap the unending work of women round you if the chill
comes over you in your fidgeting fearful fingers please knit a
nubbly prayer for me

Hospital

A prison for the housing and correcting of bodies run amok. An economy hotel of the unwilling, with the institutional stink of germ-free boiled laundry, gallons of industrial sludgefood rendered in the same giant vats. Its walls are painted with leftover porridge — don't ask what's in the lasagna. This is the barracks of regulated shit, of calibrated piss, of paper blankets, plastic pillows, of punitive starched linen. Here Death moans all night in the next bed, disturbing the thin dreams of those who sleep with one eye open.

In this bunkhouse, body parts grow monstrous in the rich soil of our dependency, as in the body image of the blind, where braille-reading fingers swell thick as limbs. Thus does the fantastic child-scribble anatomy of hospital reconfigure all proprioception. In their various wards, the thousand essential services of the body are on strike. Megalomaniac brains feed on their wild imaginings. Wombs loom like great pumpkins where Peter's put a small compliant person and kept her very well. Veins become death-curve mountain highways, hearts grow visible through chests huge and red as stop signs. Their very breathlessness inflates the importance of shallow lungs; knotted bellies swell; the flaky skin, once charred, peels off like torn book pages. The geophysical self is mapped and measured, its every tremor recorded, every reticent nook and cranny forced to speak into the microphone. The entire body buzzes and hums with monitored noise and colour.

Down the corridors of saints we dance with thin metal partners, our sole supports, our weeping coat racks. Robust doctors and nurses grope each other in the linen closet, chastised by horrified nursing sisters. Life seeks its trysts in whatever corners it can find amid the brokenness, the oozing, the drugged and the dying. Dysplastic cells grow and multiply. No chaplain forgives fast enough, no poison drip wears the rock of them away, no delicate blade pits out the countless pollen-grains of death, no fire sufficiently scorches the earth in which they seed.

Those who have talked for a living are shouted down by their long-silent cancers. Those who think are undone by a sudden clap of thoughtlessness. Those who shoulder the world are laid low by a gouty toe. Those who once wrote libraries giggle at Saturday morning cartoons. Sweet grandmothers swear like sailors and stash their shit under the bed. Those who undress in the dark and scurry shyly from showers find themselves spread-eagled naked before pimply-faced residents. Those who will never see their own marrow, who wince at a drop of their own blood, find the great meat machine of their bodies sabotaged by its tiniest cogs — fated now and for unknowable years hereafter. With constant listening to the heart, the pulse, the ticking brain, the sloshing juices, the wheezing lungs, the turbid passage of mud, the painful scrape of bone against bone, the organs of equilibrium become hypervigilant. Tendrils of attention weed through the body like ivy, a vast paranoid CIA of the flesh.

We do not wish to be here, surrounded by bizarre casualness, the appalling bonhomie of body workers for whom modesty and mystery are old news. We endure the whistling of organ miners, the baseball banter of tumour excavators, the heavy dates of blood harvesters, the hockey scores of urinal emptiers, the soap opera narrative of irrigators of wounds and dressers of purulent flesh. Through the windows of our nightmares come housebreakers with bags of criminal tools: the prybars of thermometers; the ropes and bindings of blood pressure cuffs, breathing tubes, IVs; the knives and needles, pills and powders of the junkie-thief feeding his habit; the drugging potions so we won't call the police when we wake and find the body house ransacked and the graffiti of the vandals scarred into our flesh. We suffer the well-intentioned and ignorant reassurance of tray carriers, floor moppers and linen changers, wholesome folk of a hundred foreign languages who deceive us back to a normalcy that will never be ours again. For the first time we have known betrayal by our own bodies; the virginity of our immortality can never be restored.

Disappearances

*I felt a mystical connection to the number of
confirmed dead whose names were not released.*
— *Harryette Mullen*

Becoming Invisible

I'd been long alone, the work had not gone well. Perhaps
I would walk. Something might yet materialize. I was almost
out when I heard them come up the path, the tide of their
laughter staining me when I'd hoped to slip away clean. As
someone twisted the knob from her side, I touched it from
mine and, thus joined, we opened the door together, swinging
it in to where I stood, angled, half-hidden, amid hooked
coats, empty hats and hooded slickers. My daughter's friend
stepped in. If she detected me, she was too shy to say so. She
had always found me strange and often fell into an unnatural
reticence in my presence. Then my daughter scampered up
the stairs. My wife followed, swinging the door half-heartedly
behind her. As I stepped out into the night, I heard my loved
ones calling me, and the timid friend offering, as one who
does not expect to be believed about seeing a ghost, that she
had glimpsed me standing wordless at the bottom of the stairs.
So strange did this idea sound when she said it that I think
she began to doubt it herself, and did not insist on it being so.

Whisperers

He said that with her death a unique voice had been not so
much silenced as subdued. I found this slightly unsettling,
as though he was saying the dead never die but only grow
slightly hoarse; that they never stop talking, just get harder
to make out. After that, it seemed I did hear their voices
everywhere, muttering in the laundromat, whispering on
otherwise empty buses. It became impossible to walk down a
wind-whipped street late at night without straining to figure
out just who I was hearing. Oddly, I never did hear that
unique voice of which he spoke.

Lost Shadow

Left my shadow behind in a Science Centre exhibit.
Something about phosphorescence or luminescence. It'll grow
back. It did before, after an early girlfriend pinned it to the
wall of her dorm room. Her mother found it behind the door
and remarked on its nakedness. It was a slimmer, Peter Pan
shadow then, and looked better undressed. Science feels a
poor substitute for eternal youth.

Self-loathing

I dislike men who resemble me. To spot one crossing the street is to mistake myself a moment, and think Oh God, there goes that sad poet! What an unprepossessing figure, what a shabby fat fellow he's become! He was young once, at least passably good-looking. Now he is no one, nothing, and worse yet, a dime a dozen. I see them everywhere, nosing through dusty bookshops, walking their flea-bitten dogs. Why don't they distinguish themselves, make something of their lives? I hate to confess it, but if I ever met one face-to-face, I might hit him, so insulting do I find his mere presence.

Listening

I drove north in the dark alone, deserted roads a flight path from the hive of the world. Snow fell, melted, and slicked the pavement; I was glad to hit gravel and feel earth's texture return. The radio began to crackle and fade as I pulled off the public road. On a drifted hill, I could just make out the announcer: *Now here's someone not often on air.* I stopped the car and sat a moment, curious, listening, white flakes burying me deeper in black night. The engine ticked down, grew silent and respectful, acknowledging the radio presence of Marcel Marceau.

Mysterious Disappearance

When she tells me I'll not be insured against this peril, I'm
not surprised. Who could possibly mount a bulwark against
the unfathomable? No Great West Life could calculate
appropriate compensation for being lifted bodily into
a chariot of fire beside the prophet Ezekiel. No Allstate
protects me, as I lie on the dock, wave-sound lapping into
my dreams, against being carried off in my sleeping bag
by a Sasquatch. What actuary can quantify the odds of my
vanishing, molecule by molecule, in front of horrified teachers
and children at the next school barbeque? What reasonable
consumer expects wandering-off-into-the-Amazon-jungle
insurance; developing-amnesia-after-a-fall-from-my-bike-
and-stumbling-off-to-join-the-circus-as-a-sad-faced-clown
insurance? I smile and say of course I understand completely.
Then she says, No, no, she meant the earrings, not stolen
but mislaid, the diamond dropping unheard from the ring's
golden claws. Oh, I say. I see. Clearly she has a different
notion than I of what constitutes a *classic case* of 'mysterious
disappearance.'

Late Father

He keeps popping up, refusing to stay in his box. Which was
endlessly amusing when we were kids, trying to force the
little Egyptian back into his sarcophagus, not grasping how
polarities might be covertly reversed, from *attract* to *repel.*
But every secret has its little casket and this one, a salesman's
giveaway, was intended to keep him in our chuckling father's
memory. Packing up a life, we pawed through the goods and
chattels, claiming one thing and another, this trinket among
them. The eldest took it, sheepish at the tiny grim joke that
had so mystified us. Even now, knowing the trick, we're still
suckers for a dead man who won't stay dead.

My Father's Tongue

Outside the one-room schoolhouse, he's free for an hour.
Students may lunch where they please till the sound of the
handbell. It's coming on summer. Learning stretches past
wheatfields. Over the horizon, boys may be other than
farmers; the world is larger than can be ridden across in a day.
Far away, the boys see their speck of a teacher swinging the
bell, from which they've removed the tongue. Unrestrained
laughter as they turn and disappear. This is my father's story,
but the joke is on me, because his tongue is silent. He has run
off, and the only voice I hear is my own.

My Mother's Photos

Enclosed with Mom's packet of snaps, a list of amateur
mistakes — *double exposure* heavily circled, with tips for
avoiding this error. Shopper's Drug clearly unaware that
old age bestows certain visions. Grandchildren grow from
flowerpots. Disembodied hands appear, praying, in sleeves
of fire, as another hand floats, gesturing, over a Bible. In the
grass a window, with my dead father peering out. She shrugs
off the critical list and orders duplicates for all concerned.

My Mother's Number

She's had it since long distance first wormed its way into families. Like the speed of light, my mother's phone number is a constant of the universe. Today her great-granddaughter can touch one button on a cell and summon in an eye-blink the same homely digits it seemed to take minutes to rotary. The numerals have grown larger as her sight dims but the sequence itself has endured unchanged through wars, floods, divorces, births and deaths. She's moved within and outside the neighbourhood, seen her children scatter to the far reaches of a vast, cold country, but this one string of numbers forever ties them together. In the movie π, a Kabbalistic formula for determining the name of God is mistaken for the key to making fortunes on the stock market: 453-4074 has that sort of potency for me. When my mother dies, a black hole will open up in the white pages. The phone company will retire her number, raising it to the rafters on a jersey wider than Gretsky's as her children, their children and their children's children weep at centre ice, because now none of us can ever phone home again.

My Part

I was turned down for the lead in the story of my life. Too short, they said. Too green, they said. Too fat. Too funny-looking. They were unmoved by my pleas that I'm perfect for the part, that this was the role I was born to play, that I've been playing it all my life. Naturally, I was broken-hearted. After losing this one, what other role would make sense? I pestered them for weeks, phoning them at home, accosting them in the street. Finally they softened and let me understudy. They promise to look at me again should the run be extended; maybe by then, they say, I'll have grown into the part. Meanwhile, I'm just another body in the chorus, going through the motions. Doing the same old song and dance, hoping that other hotshot dies.

Eight Items or Less

I'm in the checkout at the No Frills grocery, waiting to pay
for the sin of my appetites. It's taking an eternity. Shamed
out of Eight Items or Less and now burdened with that extra
guilt, I stand at the back of the longest line ever. Sinners all,
with so much to confess and atone for. The clerk stares into
the soul of each one and asks if that's all, sensing something
undeclared in the undercarriage of the buggy or slipped into
that dark pocket next to the heart. Why did I choose the
basket? Arms aching, I drop it to the floor and prod it forward
inch by inch with my foot. What *is* the price of betrayal, bad
parenting, failing to love my neighbour? How could I have
dreamed of slipping through the express! My sins are legion
and like discounted fruit, grow more rotten with each
passing minute.

Anonymity

In the class photo of humanity, I'm the short guy in the back row. Dressed in mud, concrete, industrial noise, I can walk down any street and vanish utterly. We've arrived at the beep, please leave a message to be ignored like all the rest. Published by So What Press and mailed directly to the dead letter department of the Milky Way Post Office, there is no hope for poetry except that hope we have for spring. A poem is a secret as safe as a single blade of grass, a grain of sand, a shard of light in the night sky. There is a dull bird whose one bright colour is on the underside of his wings. I would be that bird whose beauty is unknown to himself, unseen except in flight, and then only by the earthbound.

Acknowledgements

The author acknowledges the support of the Ontario Arts Council and its grant recommenders.

'The Landslide Effect' is a phrase from Zbigniew Herbert; "every secret has its little casket" comes from Gaston Bachelard; and "all stones are broken stones" is a line from James Richardson. 'The Big Cat Circus' would like to thank Wisława Szymborska. 'Eight Items or Less' is after Don Novello.

Various poems have appeared elsewhere, sometimes in earlier versions: 'Hospital' in *The Last Cabbage of the Morning* (Tall Tree Press, 2003), 'Skipping' in *Where Babies Come From* (Tall Tree Press, 2009) and others in *The Landslide Effect* (Tall Tree Press, 2009), *The New Quarterly*, *Dream Catcher* and *Exile*. 'Nocturnal Visitors' appeared in *Exile* and was reprinted in *Best Canadian Poetry in English 2010*.

Some of these pieces were inspired by events in the lives of others. This book is for them, with gratitude.

GLEN DOWNIE worked in cancer care for many years in Vancouver, and now lives in Toronto. In 1999, he served as Writer-in-Residence at Dalhousie University's Medical Humanities Program. He has published several collections of poetry, including *Loyalty Management* (2007), which won the Toronto Book Award.